Herbs and How to Grow Them PENN

GU00792845

Contents

Introduction

The use of herbs both in the kitchen and in medicine is a practice that stretches back into pre-history. The ancient Greeks and the Romans used them for both purposes, and every Elizabethan garden in Britain grew large quantities of herbs. Indeed, some unfortunates have even been put to death for too comprehensive a knowledge of the medicinal uses of herbs. A magical quality was attached to their use and it was a short step from a good knowledge of their healing qualities to accusations of witchcraft.

Even today, many old wives' tales still exist, particularly in the country areas of Britain, where some plants are considered to be unlucky and others to be possessed of qualities that still smack of the superstitions of the Middle Ages.

But not all herbal remedies are old wives' tales. Even today, modern medicine draws on such plants as foxglove and poppy to produce invaluable drugs.

With the possible exception of the odd sleep-inducing 'tzisane' and one or two recipes to settle overfed stomachs, however, it is wise to leave doctoring to the doctors, and to restrict the use of herbs to the kitchen.

It seems odd that, while herbs were in wide usage five hundred years ago, until very recently their popularity waned, leaving only four to hold the fort. Sage, parsley, thyme and mint are known and used in just about every British kitchen, but the use of many of the other easy-to-grow and quite delicious varieties has been neglected by all except the trendy urban housewife. That is a shame, because many have qualities as good as or even superior to our traditional favourites.

Most herbs are easy to grow, and take up little room. Many will even do well in pots on the balcony or even on the kitchen windowsill. Many are very attractive plants that will enhance the herbaceous border, while others make an eye-catching edging to the vegetable plot or a path.

Alternatively, a space can be set aside specifically for herbs. Formal herb gardens were a great favourite of the Elizabethans, and they can be copied even in modern gardens. Care must be taken, though, to select the right varieties for a formal garden. Some herbs are very invasive and will take over from less vigorous varieties, while others will grow up to 3.5m (10ft) high.

Personally, I would keep certain herbs such as parsley, mint or chives to the vegetable garden. Others, such as horseradish, need specialized treatment and are best grown in a corner on their own.

Whichever method you decide to adopt, allow a little room for experiment, not only in the growing, but in the cooking too. Once you get used to the flavour of herbs, 'plain' cooking will seem very uninteresting. As most of us who have grown even the common-or-garden mint will know, there is no flavour like that of herbs *fresh* from the garden.

Herb Mixtures

Bouquet Garni

The French, long renowned for their cuisine, have always used herbs to add distinct flavours to their food. For some dishes they use several herbs together, and this is usually done in the form of a bouquet garni.

Though this may sound like some outlandish foreign recipe, it is in fact no more than a collection of herbs tied together and hung inside the cooking pot. Mrs Beeton describes it in her usual authoritative way as 'the mainstay of French cuisine' though that is decidedly open to question. Certainly there is more to French cooking than a collection of herbs!

Traditionally, bouquet garni consists of a few sprigs of parsley, a sprig of thyme, a bay leaf and perhaps a few marjoram, basil and celery leaves. The composition can be varied, however, according to taste and the dish being prepared. A little experimentation is called for! In Provençal cooking, for example, a little orange zest is also added.

The herbs are often placed inside a muslin bag and hung inside the pot with a piece of cotton. It is used in dishes that take a long time to cook, such as casseroles and marinades. Do not forget to remove the bag before serving the dish, since the collection of herbs should on no account be eaten!

Herb Vinegar

Another way of using herbs together is in herb vinegar. This can be used in the bath, where about a cupful is added to the water. It is said to be excellent for the skin and a good relief from the pains of sunburn, since it replaces the natural oils. It can also be used in the kitchen.

6 tablespoons fresh chopped mint
3 tablespoons fresh chopped thyme
3 tablespoons fresh rosemary needles
1 litre (1¾pt) cider vinegar (malt or wine vinegar can also be used)

Wash the herbs gently, shake them and pat them dry on a clean cloth. Put them in an airtight, screw-topped jar and pour on the vinegar. Secure the top and shake vigorously. The jar should then be left for at least a fortnight, but it should be shaken vigorously every day. After a couple of weeks, the vinegar should be strained and placed in another jar. It can be kept in a decorative container in the bathroom or in the kitchen.

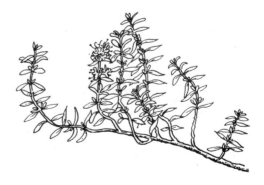

Angelica
(Angelica archangelica)

An intriguing history surrounds this vigorous herb. The name is said to derive from the archangel Michael who appeared in a vision in the 14th century to declare that the herb was a certain cure for bubonic plague.

Widely grown and collected wild in the Middle Ages, the roots of the plant were used for making medicines to 'ease the stomach' while the leaves were used in cooking and to make soothing drinks. The stems and flowers were candied, and that, indeed, is the main use of the plant today. The stems can also be chopped and added to salads, though the flavour takes a bit of getting used to.

Cultivation

Angelica is a very tall-growing perennial, though its life is short and it is best grown in the garden as a biennial. Thus, if seed is sown in late summer, the stems can be cut during June the following year. It will generally produce a number of self-sown seedlings, so once established, new plants are no problem.

It prefers a moist, rich, well-drained soil and partial shade.

It is essential to sow fresh seed, or it will not germinate. If possible, beg a little seed from a friend who grows it. That way, you can make sure that it is collected fresh and it can be sown immediately. Seed bought from a reputable seed house, however, will be kept in optimum conditions after harvesting, so germination will not be too erratic. Don't expect a very high germination. Since two plants will easily provide enough stems for the average family, there should be no practical difficulty in establishing enough plants.

Sow the seed in August, about 13mm ($\frac{1}{2}$in) deep, in their growing position. Eventually, the plants will need to be at least 1m (3ft) apart, so the seed should be sown in groups this distance apart. As soon as the seedlings are large enough to be handled, they should be thinned to leave the strongest seedling in each group. An alternative is to sow the seeds in pots or pans in the greenhouse at about the same time, and to transplant them to their flowering positions. Grown in this way, they will not generally be as large as those sown in their permanent positions.

The following year, there should be little difficulty in establishing plants, since they will seed themselves. Make sure that the young seedlings are thinned at an early stage, or they may well get out of hand.

An alternative method of growing is to cut the stems back before the plants flower. This will effectively continue the life of the plant, though it has two disadvantages.

The plants will lose vigour over three or four years, and also, the flowers will be lost.

Preservation

To make candied angelica take stems from young, healthy plants and cut them into 7.5cm (3in) lengths. Make up a brine from 8g ($\frac{1}{4}$oz) of salt to 2 litres ($3\frac{1}{2}$pt) of water. Boil the brine and pour it over the stems. Leave it for 10 minutes and then drain. Rinse the stems in cold water and then boil them in water for a further 7 or 8 minutes until they are tender. Drain them and scrape off the skin.

Weigh the stems and make up a syrup of sugar and water using equal weights of sugar and angelica. For each 450g (1lb) of sugar, use 500ml (1pt) of water. Bring the syrup to the boil and pour it over the stems. Leave the mixture to steep for 24 hours. Then drain off the syrup and repeat the process with fresh syrup made in the same way. The whole process of covering and leaving for 24 hours should be done four times. The final steeping should be for two weeks. Then drain off the syrup and leave the stems to dry on paper in a warm, dry spot for two or three days. When they are thoroughly dry, store in airtight jars.

Uses

Shoots and flowers can be candied and used in confectionery, the stems and leaves can be added to salads, and the roots are used with juniper berries to flavour gin. The seeds can also be utilized in the making of vermouth, chartreuse and some muscatel wines.

Balm
(Melissa officianalis)

The ancients considered balm to be the basis of the Elixir of Life, while later it became recognized as an excellent nerve tonic. It was also considered good for the memory, a heart stimulant, and an ideal spirit raiser—a noble herb indeed!

Nowadays, it is used in the kitchen to flavour a wide variety of dishes, and in pot-pourri for its strong lemon scent. It also attracts bees, and bee-keepers use it to rub on the inside of hives to prevent bees from swarming. A bushy, hardy perennial, this close relative of mint also produces runners, so it is easy to colonize. In fact, it may need to be checked from time to time, especially if it is growing in a herb garden with other less vigorous plants.

The plant is compact and bushy early on, but as soon as it starts to produce its rather insignificant flowers, it tends to sprawl and look messy.

Cultivation

It prefers a semi-shaded position, with a moist root-run. Don't bury it in a dark corner, though, or the leaves will blanch too much.

Sow seeds outside in April, or buy a plant to set outside in the spring. Make sure that the plant does not go short of water in the summer, and cut it back in the autumn to retain its bushy habit. It may be necessary to remove self-sown seedlings as they appear, or they will become very invasive.

The plants can also be increased by division of the roots. Simply lift one of the crowns and remove the small offsets from the outside, discarding the older centre.

Balm plants will also do well in pots and in tubs, where they will grow quite happily for many years, especially if they are fed with a liquid manure from time to time in the growing season.

Preserving

Balm is not a good subject for drying, but it does freeze well. For short-term storage, simply pack a few sprigs into a polythene bag and put it in the freezer. If you wish to keep the leaves longer, they must be blanched in boiling water for a minute. Then dip them into cold water, dry them well and put them into polythene bags for the freezer.

Uses

Balm is best used early on in the season, since later the leaves tend to lose their lemon flavour. They also go a bit stringy.

The leaves are often used in stuffings for chicken or duck, and in sausages. They can also be used in sauces, especially for fish dishes.

The young leaves are excellent chopped and added to salads, but later in their lives they tend to be indigestible.

A few leaves added to fruit before it is cooked will give it a slight lemon flavour. Finely chopped and added to vegetables just before serving, it gives a subtle freshness.

The lemon flavour is often utilized by adding the leaves to tea, and this infusion is reputed to bring down temperatures.

Basil

Sweet Basil
(Ocimum basilicum labiatae)
Bush Basil
(Ocimum minimum)

A useful herb this, especially for those inclined to over-indulgence. According to the old herbalists, it settles the stomach after an excessive intake of alcohol, prevents vomiting and nausea and is an excellent nerve tonic. Like the advice, it should be taken with a pinch of salt.

It is, however, quite superb as a flavouring for many dishes and, even though it is not easy to grow, should not be excluded from the herb garden. Though a native of India, it has been grown in Europe for about 2,000 years and has rich associations with witchcraft, superstition and religion. It is even said to drive away flies.

Sweet basil is taller growing than bush basil and is more productive. Bush basil is very well suited to cultivation in pots or tubs either inside on the kitchen windowsill or outside on the patio or balcony. Since it is subject to frost damage, this is probably the best way to grow it.

Basil seeds can be sown in peat blocks

Cultivation
Sweet basil is grown in this country as an annual, due to its dislike of low temperatures. It must ꜰᴇ ɢʀᴏᴡɴ ꜰᴏ ᴀ ꜱᴜɴɴy ꜱʜᴇʟᴛᴇʀᴇᴅ ꜱᴘᴏᴛ in rich soil and pampered like a baby.

Sow in peat pots or blocks in the greenhouse or on the window-sill in March. Harden off and plant out about 20cm (8in) apart when all danger of frost has passed in late May or early June. Alternatively, buy hardened off plants in June.

Keep the plants well watered and pinch off flower buds as they appear or growth will slow right down. Harvest the leaves for use when required.

In September, lift a few plants and pot them up. Cut them back hard and bring them into the heated greenhouse or the kitchen. They will produce another crop of leaves for at least a few months.

Bush basil can be grown in pots inside since this is a dwarf variety. The leaves are smaller, however, and so the plant is not so productive.

Drying
The dried leaves are less pungent and flavoursome than they are when fresh, but they are better than none at all. Remove the leaves when they are young and fresh, discarding any brown, discoloured or diseased ones. Hang them in a warm, dry place away from strong sunlight. When they are quite dry, crumble them and put them into airtight jars.

Basil can also be frozen, and the best way to do this is in cubes. Wash the leaves and chop them into pieces. Pack them tightly into the ice-cube tray and top up with water. Freeze them, empty them out and pack them into polythene bags for storage. When defrosted, they can be used as fresh leaves. Leaves can also be preserved by layering them with salt in jars, or in olive oil.

Uses
Include basil in all egg dishes—scrambled egg, quiches, omelettes etc. It is also particularly good with tomatoes and with mushrooms. Place basil leaves on fresh, sliced tomatoes and make them a basis for a really delicious salad. Alternatively, use them to add a rare piquancy to tomato or mushroom soups. It is also used to flavour fish and meat and will add interest to rice dishes.

Bay
(Laurus nobilis)

Bay was the plant used by the Greeks and Romans to make laurel wreaths. The plant we call laurel *(Prunus laurocerasus)* is poisonous and should not be used for cooking. If in doubt, break a leaf and smell it. Bay has a pungent smell, while laurel is practically odourless.

The plant is a native of the Mediterranean and is not entirely hardy in this country, though it can be grown outside in warmer parts.

Cultivation

Because it is frost-tender, this is not an easy plant to grow. It has a habit, in its early years, of simply turning brown and withering away for no apparent reason. It generally prefers a fairly dry, semi-shaded position, and it dislikes being moved, so if it is established in the garden, leave it alone. Perhaps a better way of growing bay is in tubs. Plants are often grown in this way and trained to formal shapes by pinching and tying young shoots. The great advantage with this method is that the plants can be brought inside for the winter,

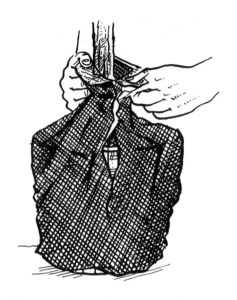

Wrap the tubs in sacking to protect the roots from frost

and so have a much greater chance of survival. If the tubs have to be left outside during the winter, the roots are even more prone to frost damage than those planted in the open ground. They must therefore be protected by wrapping with sacking, an old blanket or a layer of straw.

Plants can also be 'dwarfed' by root pruning from time to time. This way they can be grown in the kitchen.

To buy a trained tree in a tub is an extremely expensive way of acquiring a bay. It is fine if you need it for decorative purposes, because formal shapes are not easy to achieve. But if the plants are being used to provide flavouring for the kitchen, it is far better to buy a small plant and grow it on in its natural shape. Even better, beg a few cuttings from a friend.

Cuttings should be taken in late summer, using half-ripe shoots about 10cm (4in) long. Remove the bottom leaves and trim the cutting just below a leaf joint. The top should also be trimmed, this time just above a joint. Dip the bottom of the cuttings into rooting hormone and set them round the edge of a pot of sandy compost. Cover the pots with a polythene bag to retain moisture, and, ideally, place it where it can get a little gentle bottom heat. Cuttings are rather shy to root, so many more should be taken than are wanted. Once the cuttings are rooted, pot them on into individual pots.

Preserving

Bay leaves can readily be dried, and they will last in this condition for a very long time. Simply pick the leaves individually or cut some sprigs and lay them out in a cool, airy place out of direct sunlight. When dry, pack into airtight jars.

Uses

Bay leaves are almost as good dried as they are fresh. Before using fresh ones, be sure to break the leaves to release the pungent aroma. The leaves are not good to eat and should be used purely as a flavouring. Take them out of dishes before serving; they will have imparted enough flavour in any case.

Bay can be used in a wide variety of dishes. It is particularly popular in casseroles and stews, in sauces and cooked with roast meat. It is excellent with most vegetables, especially Jerusalem artichokes, giving them a subtly different flavour. Some cooks also use them in sweet dishes such as milk custards and rice.

Borage
(Borago officinalis)

Borage is without doubt the most popular of the herbalists' remedies for depression. It is a great uplifter of the heart and said to 'make a man merry and joyful'. Drunk in wine, Gerard said that 'it makes men and women glad and merry, driving away all sadness and dullness'. But then perhaps that was the effect of the wine!

Today, it is used for its delightful cucumber flavour, in summer drinks and in salads.

It is a handsome hardy annual, that in good soil will reach about 60cm (2ft) high. It bears great arching sprays of flowers of intense blue. It is worth growing as a cottage garden plant even if it is not used in the kitchen. It has the added advantage that it attracts bees.

Cultivation

Borage prefers a sunny, open situation. It is quite fussy about its position, and will not do well in shade, but fortunately, it seems to thrive in almost any soil.

Sow the seeds outside in April where they are to flower. It is best to sow in 'stations' about 38cm (15in) apart, thinning to one seedling as soon as the plants are large enough to handle.

Though the plants will, being annuals, die down at the end of the year, they will almost certainly seed themselves quite liberally. It is more likely that plants will need thinning than that they will have to be re-sown.

Preservation

The leaves of borage do not dry well, though they can be frozen in the way recommended for balm.

The flowers can be crystallized for use as sweetmeats or for decoration. They will retain their colour and, especially if preserved, will keep for several months. For short-term preserving, simply paint the flowers with beaten egg-white, and dip them into caster sugar. Dry them on a wire cake rack for 24 hours before use.

For storage over a much longer period, the flowers are crystallized in a solution of gum arabic and rose water. Put 3 teaspoons of gum arabic crystals into a jar with 3 tablespoons of rose water. Leave the solution for about 3 days, shaking from time to time until the mixture becomes sticky and glue-like. Paint the flowers carefully with the solution and dust them with caster sugar. Put them on a wire rack and leave them to dry for 24 hours. When they are quite dry place them in airtight jars for storage.

Uses

Borage is traditionally used to float on the top of long summer drinks. It is an obligatory ingredient of real Pimms No 1.

The leaves can be used in salads, though they tend to become stringy when they are older. They also bear tiny spikes, so it is important to wash them before eating.

They can be used in tea infusions, and some gardeners plant them as companion plants with strawberries, swearing that both plants grow better together.

To preserve borage flowers, paint them with egg white, then dip them in caster sugar

Chervil
(Anthriscus cerefolium)

No good cook can afford to be without chervil. It has been grown in Britain since Roman times and over the years has achieved a great reputation. Unlike most herbs, a great deal will be needed, for it can be used in quantity in soups and as a flavouring for many dishes. Don't be put off by its looks. There are few herbs which look so insignificant—rather like a weedy version of parsley—but which are so useful in gourmet cookery. It is not so popular here as our 'top four', perhaps because it has achieved a reputation of being quite difficult to grow. Given the right conditions, however, nothing could be easier.

Cultivation
Chervil has one fault. It has a habit of running to seed as soon as the weather becomes dry, or if the roots are deprived of moisture. For this reason, it is essential to grow it in a semi-shaded situation with a moisture-retentive soil. Water it by hand if necessary; it is well worth it.

This is an annual plant, so seed must be sown every year or even twice a year. If left to flower, it will conveniently seed itself.

Sow outside where it is to grow from February to April. This will supply leaves for the summer. As soon as the leaves begin to lose their fresh green appearance, it is wise to sow again. Picking will usually start in six to eight weeks. A final sowing can be made in August or September to provide leaves for the winter and spring. These sowings should be protected with cloches in all but the most temperate areas.

Alternatively, plants can be potted up and placed in a cool

greenhouse or on the kitchen windowsill.

When the plant is growing, all flowers should be picked off as soon as they are seen. This will delay seeding and extend the period of harvesting. Pull the leaves from the outside of the plant so that new ones will be continually produced from the centre of the plant.

Unless you intend to make a permanent patch of chervil, when the plants can be left to seed themselves, it is as well to allow a few plants to run to seed, so as to provide viable seed for resowing. As with angelica, the seed must be fresh when sown or it may well not germinate.

Preservation

Chervil can be dried in the normal way. Pick the leaves when they are young, discarding any that are brown, and hang them in an airy spot away from direct sunlight. When dry, crumble them and put them into airtight jars.

The leaves will also freeze well. For short-term storage, simply pack them into polythene bags and freeze them. For a longer period in store, blanch them first in boiling water for two minutes, dip them into cold water and then freeze. They can also be frozen in ice cubes.

Uses

Chervil has a spicy, mildly aniseed flavour that adds a touch of freshness wherever it is used. Try it with new potatoes for a flavour equal to or even better than mint. It can also be used chopped fresh and sprinkled on vegetables just before they are served, in egg dishes, salads, soups and sauces. Worked into butter and chilled, it makes a fine accompaniment to steak or fish. The French use it to make a chervil soup which is nothing short of supreme.

Cloches provide protection for young plants

Chives
(Allium schoenoprasum)

This milder member of the onion family is one of our more popular herbs. It has many uses, and obliges the cook by thriving on constant cutting. Indeed, it tends to deteriorate if it is not given a periodic short back and sides.

It has a variety of forms, some of them growing to 60cm (2ft) though these taller types have little advantage over their shorter cousins except perhaps that they produce more leaf for the area of soil used. The leaves tend to be coarser, though, so the shorter types are to be preferred.

A hardy perennial, chives will grow in most garden soils and is undemanding about position, if it is not deprived of moisture.

Cultivation

Being short, compact and bushy, chives make excellent edging plants for paths. They are quite attractive if allowed to flower, but tend to lose vigour if this is allowed. They can be started from seed sown outside in March or April, but quicker results are obtained by dividing the numerous bulbs that each plant produces. Even if only one plant is bought in the first place, there will soon be many more than can be used.

Plant the bulbs in spring or autumn, setting them in small clumps about 30cm (1ft) apart. The plants should be lifted, divided and replanted on a fresh piece of ground every three years, or the clumps will tend to lose vigour and deteriorate.

Plants can also be grown in pots in a cool greenhouse or in the kitchen. If a few pots are kept in different temperatures, they should produce enough leaves for use all the year round.

Though the plants are decorative in flower, looking rather like common thrift, flowering causes the plants to deteriorate, so flowers should be picked off as they appear.

Clumps should be cut in suc-cession, cutting all the leaves from the clump, down to about 13mm ($\frac{1}{2}$in) of soil level. They will soon produce masses of new leaves.

Preserving
Leaves of chives cannot be dried, but they will freeze quite well. Chop up the leaves and pack them closely into an ice-cube tray. Top up with water and freeze. When they are needed, they are taken out, defrosted in a strainer and used as fresh.

Uses
Chives are not used for cooking, since this destroys their flavour, but they can be used fresh in a variety of ways. Perhaps the most popular is to chop up the leaves and mix them with cottage or cream cheese to give a delicate onion flavour.

They add a certain something to baked jacket potatoes, and in Scotland they are traditionally used to flavour mashed potatoes that are past their best in May and June.

They are also widely used in salads and soups (especially vichyssoise), savoury spreads, pancakes and cheese sauces. Add them also to vinaigrette for an extra-special flavour.

Finally, there is an unexpected bonus from this versatile plant. When the bulbs are lifted and divided, any surplus can be pickled in wine vinegar to make really deli-cious cocktail onions.

Dill
(Anethum graveolens)

It is a pity that dill has become irrevocably associated with dill-water, an infusion made with the herb and used for centuries to assist babies to bring up wind. Though this herb has long been used medicinally as an aid to digestion, its culinary properties are without question more attractive. Its flavour is difficult to describe, being something of a paradox. A faint hint of caraway combines with a refreshing sharpness but with a slight touch of sweetness. A mystery indeed!

A feathery-leaved annual, it should be grown a little apart from fennel, since it is easily mistaken for it in appearance.

Cultivation

Dill likes a dryish, sunny situation. Sow the seeds in spring where they are to grow, and thin the resulting seedlings to about 30cm (1ft) apart. If you intend to allow the plants to flower so as to collect the seed, further sowings can be made during the spring and summer to ensure a succession. Alternatively, pinch out the flowers as they show, to encourage the production of more leaves. The leaves should also be cut fre-

quently for use, to ensure the production of plenty of young growth.

Though dill can be grown in pots and window boxes, it is seldom very successful or long-lived in those situations.

Preservation

Pick leaves when they are still young, spread them out and place them in a warm, dry, airy place out of direct sunlight.

When they are dry and brittle, crumble them and store them in airtight jars, preferably in the dark so that they retain their colour.

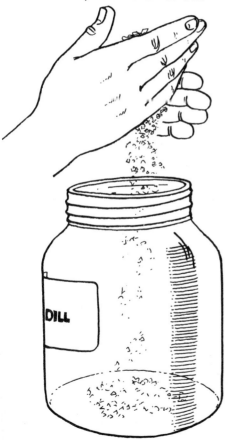

Alternatively, they can be stored in salt. Place a layer of leaves in a jar, cover with salt, and then add another layer of leaves. Continue until the jar is full, cover and store.

The seeds must be collected before they fall to the ground. Pull the plants when the flower heads turn brown, and tie them into bunches. Hang them in an airy, sunny place over a cloth or bowl to catch the seeds as they fall. When the flowerheads are quite dry, the remaining seed can be shaken out and stored in airtight jars.

Dill can also be frozen in ice cubes as described previously (p. 17).

Herb enthusiasts have for centuries used infusions of dill to help insomnia, and many still swear to its effectiveness. It is certainly an aid to digestion and for that reason, the seeds are used to flavour pickled cucumbers. Dill vinegar can easily be made by simply hanging a bunch of dill in a bottle of vinegar.

The herb is also used as a flavouring for many foods such as fish, cheese and egg dishes, sauerkraut, chicken and meat as well as salads and soups. It will also add a delicate flavour to salads.

The Russians use it widely in sour cream dishes, and it makes a fine flavouring for new potatoes— a subtle variation from the popular mint so widely used in Britain.

The seeds are often used in vegetable dishes that are cooked with little water. Crushed into shredded cabbage or cauliflower before it is steamed, it will add a delicious extra zest.

19

Fennel
(Foeniculum vulgare)

This is a vigorous hardy perennial, not to be confused with Florence fennel which is grown for its swollen stem bases. It is another herb that has been grown for thousands of years and therefore has a number of dubious attributes. It is, for example, credited with increasing the flow of mother's milk, and 'making the fat grow gaunt and

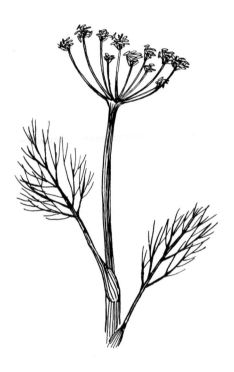

lank'. It is a vigorous, graceful perennial whose feathery foliage and bright yellow flowers (which often exceed 15cm (6in) across), will enhance any garden.

Left alone, it will grow to a pro-digious 1.5m (5ft), but since a great deal will be needed for the kitchen, this is unlikely to happen. Bear it in mind, though, if the plant is to be part of a herb garden.

Cultivation
Fennel will grow in most soils and situations provided it has plenty of sun. Make sure that the soil is fairly fertile before sowing or planting, because it will have a useful life of up to five years.

Sow in spring and thin the seedlings to about 60cm (2ft) apart. It will self-seed each year, and these seedlings can be used to transplant.

It is best to keep the plants away from coriander and caraway in case cross-pollination occurs. They should also be kept away from dill. When the leaves are required, some stems should be cut back hard to encourage new young growth. Fennel responds well to pot-growing if it is kept cut back quite hard.

Preservation
The leaves, stems and seeds can all be dried for storage, although the leaves tend to lose some of their flavour and aroma. Pick the leaves and stems when they are young and hang them in a dry, airy, warm place out of direct sunlight. When they are dry, crumble the leaves and pack them into airtight jars. The stems should be wrapped in foil.

To store seed, cut the stems before the flowers drop their seed and hang them upside down in bunches over a cloth. When they are quite dry, shake out the remainder of the seed.

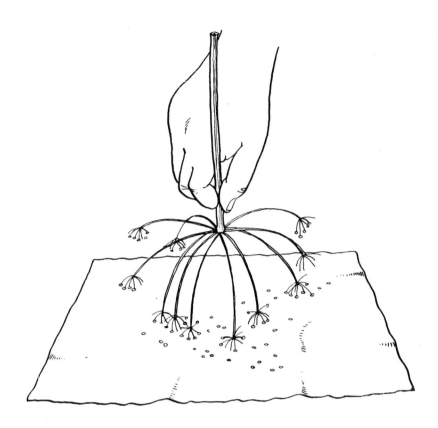

Collecting fennel seeds

The stems and leaves can also be frozen. They will keep longer if they are blanched in boiling water for a couple of minutes, plunged into cold water and packed into polythene bags before freezing.

Uses

Fennel has a pleasant aniseed flavour that will add a touch of freshness to many dishes.

The seeds possess the strongest flavour and these are pounded and used in sweet as well as savoury dishes. They make a pleasant accompaniment to cooked apples and can be sprinkled on fresh fruit. They are also used in bread, biscuits and cakes. The seeds can be used to make an infusion which is said to be an effective aid to the digestion.

The leaves can be used in salads, with fish dishes, poultry and meat. They can also be chopped and served in soups and vinaigrettes, as well as on vegetables just before serving.

The stems can be burnt under fish to impart the aniseed flavour —a popular Italian method.

It is also said that seeds chewed whole will abate hunger, so they could be a valuable aid to slimming!

Garlic
(Allium sativum)

This herb is either loved or hated, often depending upon whether you have eaten it or simply had it breathed over you. Eat mutton with a French family and you may become addicted. The cure is to travel on the French metro!

It has been used for centuries and, like most herbs, is accredited with strange powers. The Romans and Egyptians believed that it imparted strength, and fed it in quantity to their soldiers and labourers. The Indians believe it to be associated with the devil and won't touch it.

In Britain, where many country folk still swear by it, it has been used to cure pimples and to aid the digestion. Indeed, it is still often credited with the power to prolong life to a very old age. In the Middle Ages, it was also thought to have the power to deter vampires.

Cultivation

Garlic is not difficult to grow, though it prefers a light, well-drained soil with plenty of organic matter. A sunny spot is essential.

The garlic bulb consists of several separate cloves, which should be split up before planting. In milder areas they can be planted in November, but elsewhere March is better. Set them about 2.5cm (1in) deep and 15cm (6in) apart. They are best planted in drills and then covered, rather than pressing them into the soil, which tends to compact the earth underneath

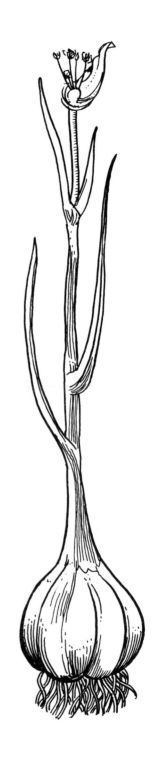

them. Keep them weed-free during the season, and never let them go short of water. If any small mauve flowers appear, pinch them out immediately.

Preserving
Harvest the bulbs when the foliage goes yellow and dies down. This is normally during July or early August. Lift the bulbs carefully with a fork, rather than tugging them out which may damage the stem and cause rotting. Leave the bulbs outside for a few days to dry, and then store them in a dry, airy, frost-free spot, either in nets or in open trays. Put a few of the best bulbs on one side for replanting next autumn or spring.

Uses
Above all, remember that garlic is a very powerful herb and an anti-social one at that. Even a little makes for pretty unpleasant breath! But, to the devotee, it is unequalled as a flavouring herb.

Rub a clove of garlic around the salad bowl before use, and that will be sufficient to impart quite a strong flavour. It can also be used with most meat dishes and with fish. When it is cooked whole, it does not impart anything like the unpleasant odour associated with fresh cloves.

It can also be pressed in a special garlic press, and the juice used in sauces, in salad dressings and on crusty bread.

A favourite continental method of use is to suspend the cloves in a bottle of olive oil and vinegar to add a special flavour.

Planting cloves of garlic

23

Horseradish
(Armoracia rusticana)

A very hardy perennial that grows wild in many parts of the British Isles. When well grown, however, it has longer roots of a much better flavour, so it is worth growing some in the garden.

Horseradish was once grown almost exclusively for medicinal purposes. It was claimed that it prevented scurvy and alleviated rheumatism. It was also said to be a good cure for chilblains.

The leaves contain poisons and should not be eaten, but the roots contain them in such small amounts that it would need hundredweights to do any harm.

Success with horseradish is virtually assured. Indeed, it could well take over the garden if left to its own devices.

Cultivation

Pieces of root (known as 'thongs') should be planted the right way up in March. Set them about 30cm (1ft) apart each way. Select a piece of ground that was manured for a previous crop, or that has been enriched with well-rotted compost or peat. The addition of manure could make the roots fork, and they are then difficult to prepare. Give them a sunny spot, and cultivate the soil deeply, since the roots will go down a long way.

During the season, there is very little to do, since the plants will compete easily with most weeds.

In October, the roots will be ready for lifting and storing. Some authorities suggest that the beds should be cleared every three or even four years. In my opinion, the best way of preventing the roots

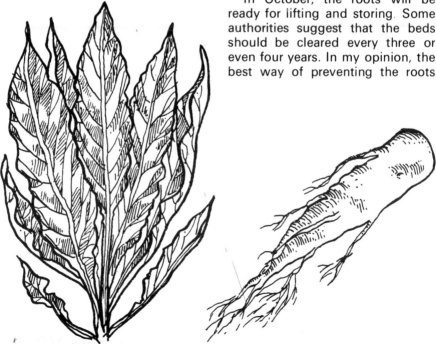

from becoming invasive is to lift the lot every year and to replant the following year. This will not have any effect on the size of the crop.

Save a few thongs for replanting the following spring. These should be stored in boxes of sand during the winter. In the spring, the stored roots will start to sprout, and are then ready for replanting.

Preservation
Roots can be stored in the same way as any root vegetable—in boxes of sand, peat or soil. The roots can also be grated and pickled. To pickle, wash the roots first in hot water and scrape off the skin. Grate the flesh and pack it tightly into screw-topped jars.

They should then be covered with salted vinegar, using 1 teaspoonful of salt to each 250ml ($\frac{1}{2}$pint) of vinegar. Seal the jars tightly and store in a cool place.

Uses
The most popular use for horseradish is in a sauce used to accompany beef. This is a particularly popular Jewish dish. It can be used in the same way with fish.

A delightful sauce can be made by mixing freshly grated horseradish into a mayonnaise of cream and olive oil with a little lemon juice added.

A gourmet sauce for use with baked trout is made by mixing grated horseradish, walnuts and sour cream.

To make horseradish cream, mix a little mustard, salt and pepper and a good pinch of sugar into 125ml ($\frac{1}{4}$pint) of thick cream. Add two tablespoons of grated horseradish and one tablespoon of white vinegar.

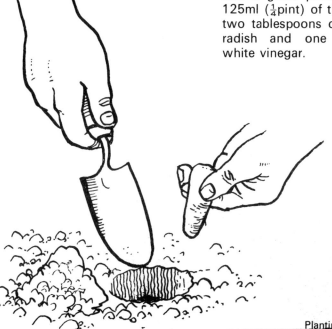

Planting horseradish roots

25

Juniper
(Juniperus communis)

The common juniper is one of our three native conifers, and many are to be found growing wild on the chalk downs of the south of England. It is also widely distributed throughout the world. Its awl-shaped leaves are silver-backed and prickly to the touch, and it makes a handsome background to other herbs, and especially to silver-leaved plants. It thrives in windswept, generally inhospitable conditions, so it should be possible to grow it almost anywhere, though it does prefer a chalky soil.

The whole plant is aromatic, especially when the leaves are crushed.

The berries, which are used for culinary purposes, are green at first and take two or three years to ripen to the black colour necessary before they can be used in the kitchen. While they are ripening, however, new berries are being formed, so after the first crop, there will be an annual succession.

Oil of juniper is a well-known ingredient of medicines used for kidney and digestive troubles.

Cultivation

In order to ensure berries, it is necessary to have both a male and a female plant, since it is unisexual and only very rarely do male and female flowers bloom on the same plant. The female flowers are small green cones, while the male flowers are green catkins.

Though juniper can be propagated from seed, plants raised in this way will take many years to reach the berrying stage, so it is better to buy plants from a nurseryman.

Ideally, plant them in a sunny position in soil that has been limed if necessary. Apart from keeping the plants free from weeds, there is very little to do once they are established.

Preservation

Pick berries only when they are ripe and black. To dry them, place the berries separately on trays at room temperature. It is necessary for the process to be very slow and gentle, so resist the temptation to put them in the oven to hurry the process along. When they have shrivelled slightly and lost their moisture, put them into airtight jars for storage.

The berries can also be frozen. Place them on a tray so that they are not touching each other, and freeze them. Then pack them into polythene bags and replace them in the freezer. Do not freeze them in the bags or they will stick together and be difficult to separate.

Uses

Perhaps the best-known use for juniper berries is in the manufacture of gin, but this is, of course, only a commercial process. In the kitchen, they are used generally to flavour strong dishes such as hare, rabbit, venison and quail, and they are also used in stuffings for chicken and turkey.

Before use, they should be crushed in a mortar or with the back of a wooden spoon to bring out the astringent, bitter-sweet flavour. Bear in mind that berries ripened in relatively sunless situations will be less flavoursome than those ripened in full sun, so you may need more. It is best always to experiment with a small quantity first.

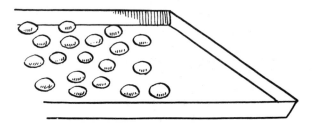

Lovage
(Levisticum officinale)

A noble plant indeed, and, sadly, not grown often enough in this country. Given good soil conditions, it can grow to a majestic 2m (6ft), so allow it plenty of room in the herb garden. It is unlikely that more than one plant will be needed in the kitchen, so it's worth finding it a place.

Lovage is reputed to be an import from ancient Rome, brought here as a cure for rheumatic ills. It has achieved a great medicinal reputation, being recommended by the old herbalists for every variety of disorder from bladder troubles to jaundice. Now, thankfully perhaps, its use is confined to the kitchen, though even today medical men are looking into the old herbalists' claims for this plant among many others.

Cultivation

Lovage hates poor, dry soil, so plant it in well-worked, moist soil into which generous quantities of organic matter have been incorporated.

It is easy to raise this plant from seed, preferably sown as soon as it is ripe. It will, however, be at least a year before plants raised in this way can be used, so it is perhaps best to buy a plant from a nurseryman.

Set plants at least 60cm (2ft) apart. Once established, new plants can be provided, if necessary, by lifting and dividing the fleshy roots.

Keep the plants weed-free, and in dry weather pay particular attention to watering. If they are being grown for the leaves and stems, cut back the flower stalks that arise strongly from the centre of the plant, to encourage the production of fresh young leaves.

This plant is not really suitable for pots, window-boxes or tubs, since the roots will rapidly outgrow their accommodation.

Preserving

Lovage will dry quite well. Use fresh young leaves, gathered before the plant has a chance to flower. Tie them in bunches and hang them in an airy, warm place, away from direct sunlight. When the leaves are dry, crumble them and pack them into airtight jars for storage.

If the seeds are to be kept, the flower heads should be gathered before they shed the seed. Hang them upside-down over a cloth, and shake out the seed when it is dry. Store in airtight jars.

Alternatively, the chopped leaves can be frozen in ice-cube trays and then packed into polythene bags.

Uses

All parts of the plant can be used for flavouring. The leaves have a delicious flavour of hot, peppery celery, and the flavour is quite strong, so they should be used sparingly. Again, experiment with a small quantity first. Chop the leaves into salads or wipe the leaves over meat before roasting and put a few around the joint while cooking.

It is greatly valued in soups, stews and casseroles and in stewed meat dishes generally. When the leaves are cooked in this way, a rather more generous helping can be used.

The young stems are cut into short lengths and used in vegetable and poultry dishes that are to be cooked in water.

The crushed seeds are also used in biscuits, cakes and bread to give a spicy flavour, and the stems can be candied in the same way as angelica (though it has a different flavour entirely).

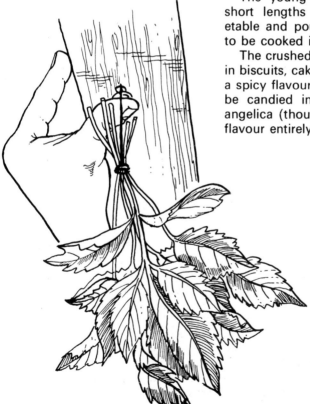

Marjoram

Pot Marjoram
(Origanum onites)
Sweet Marjoram
(Origanum majorana)
Wild Marjoram or Oregano
(Origanum vulgare)

A widely used herb with a great versatility, marjoram was recognized as a herb to induce happiness. It was spread on the floor of the bridal chamber where its sweet perfume helped to counteract the fumes of briars, burnt to drive away evil spirits. Boiled in water, it was said that it 'easeth such as are given to much sighing'. For the gourmet, it certainly does spread happiness, because its sweet, spicy flavour will transform many dishes that would otherwise lack flavour.

There are, in fact, three types of marjoram used in the kitchen.

Pot marjoram is a perennial with erect, reddish stems and small leaves. The pale pink or white flowers make it an attractive plant for the border. It is the easiest of the three to grow, but unfortunately is the least flavoursome.

Sweet marjoram is really only

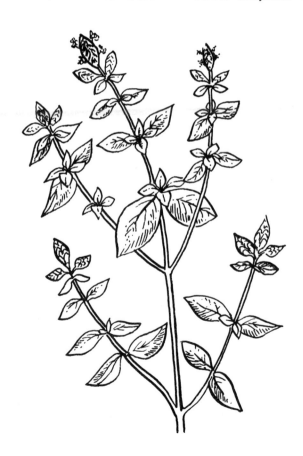

half-hardy, though in favoured areas it may be possible to keep it through the winter. It is the most aromatic and flavoursome of the three. The flower buds contain the truly delightful flavour of this herb, but the flowers themselves are insignificant and are best removed.

Oregano is the peasant of the family. Its flavour is strong and penetrating, and so it should be used with discretion. It is often used in exotic, spicy dishes from Italy, Spain and South America.

Cultivation

All the marjorams like a well-drained soil and a very sunny spot. Make sure, before planting or sowing, that the soil has plenty of well-rotted manure or compost worked into it to retain moisture.

All types can be raised from seed sown in the spring. The seed is very fine, so it should not be covered too deeply. It is wise to mix it with a little sand before sowing to ensure that growth is not too thick.

Alternatively, plants can be raised from cuttings or division of the roots in the spring.

At the end of the summer, a few plants can be potted up and brought into the house or greenhouse to provide a winter supply. They will grow well in pots inside, but will thrive only in a position of full sun.

Preserving

Marjoram dries very well, though since pot marjoram will keep some of its leaves in winter, it is hardly worth it. Sweet marjoram is particularly good and its flavour will

strengthen on drying. It is essential to cut at the right time—just as the buds are about to open into flower. Oregano is also good for drying, but it must be remembered that the flavour will be extremely strong.

Cut the stems (leaving a few to continue the good work), tie them up into bundles and hang them in a warm, airy spot away from direct sun.

All types will also freeze well in polythene bags. For longer storage, blanch the stems first.

Uses

Use marjoram in all dishes that may otherwise have a bland flavour. It is used in meat, fish and egg dishes, sausage-meat and stuffings. It is particularly good chopped small and sprinkled on vegetables just before serving, and it will make an amazing difference to salads.

Mint

Apple Mint *(Mentha rotundi-folia*—Bowles variety)
Spearmint *(Mentha spicata)*

One of the oldest herbs in use, and one of our most popular, mint is considered obligatory with roast lamb, with new potatoes and with peas.

It was certainly grown by the Ancient Romans, and it was used by athletes of latter days to strengthen nerves and sinews. It was and is still used by country folk, who rub it into the skin to prevent the attentions of insects.

But it is in the kitchen that it really comes into its own.

There are several types of mint in cultivation, some of them grown purely for their fragrance. Apple mint and spearmint are certainly the most useful in cooking. Apple mint has the further advantage that it is resistant to rust disease, which may attack spearmint and several of the other varieties, rendering them useless in the kitchen.

Apple mint has large, rounded, hairy leaves, while the leaves of spearmint are smaller and thinner. When planting apple mint, bear in mind that it is vigorous and can grow to 1½m (5ft) tall, and that both have an invasive habit.

Cultivation
Mint prefers a moist soil and will do well in shade, though the flavour tends to be better in full sun.

Their greatest disadvantage is that they are very invasive and can quickly swamp a herb garden. The best way to control their growth is to plant in a container. A large pot or tub sunk into the ground with the rim a little above soil level is ideal. They will also do quite well in large pots inside.

The best way to propagate the plants is either to buy one plant and later lift and replant a few of the strong growing rhizomes, or to beg a root from a friend.

At the end of the season, lift a root, cut a few rhizomes into short lengths and set them in a box of compost. They can then be brought inside where they will soon shoot to provide fresh young leaves all the winter.

Preserving
Mint leaves dry well, though it is debatable whether it is worth doing so, since dried leaves lose

Plant rhizomes in a box of compost

some of their flavour, and the plants can be forced so easily. If you do want to dry some, pick a few stems, tie them into bundles and hang them in a warm airy spot out of direct sunlight. The leaves can also be frozen fresh in ice cube trays.

Uses

Though the most common use for mint in Britain is with lamb, peas and potatoes, it will also make a remarkable difference to the flavour of other young vegetables. Carrots and turnips are particularly improved, the mint seemingly intensifying the natural flavour of the vegetables. Mint leaves can also be added to tomatoes and mushrooms when they are grilled, and is particularly good in salads.

With lamb, mint is generally used in a jelly or sauce, but the meat will be even further improved if it is stuffed with fresh mint before cooking.

Leaves can also be infused to make mint tea, and the fresh young leaves make a pleasant addition to fruit drinks and cock-tails.

Parsley
(Petroselinum crispum)

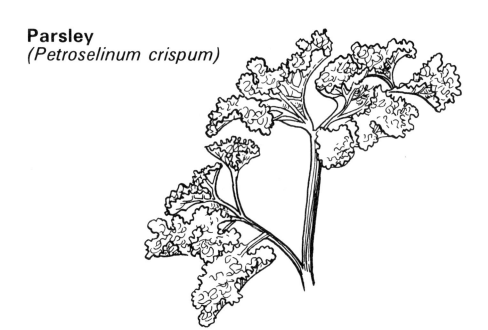

Undoubtedly our most popular and widely used herb. Time was when there was no need to grow it because the butcher would always oblige with a bunch from his window display. Today, with the advent of the plastic variety, we need to grow our own.

Parsley is notoriously difficult to germinate, and this fact alone has surrounded it in mystery. Some say that its slowness to show is because it must 'go nine times back to the Devil', while others are adamant that 'a man must make his wife sow parsley'. What a bachelor does they don't say! It is also said that only an honest man can grow it, and that 'he who grows it well will have no sons and only barren daughters'. It is certainly rich in vitamin C and is said to 'cleanse the blood', though what that means is unclear.

Cultivation
Parsley grows best on fertile, well-drained soil, and will do best in partial shade. It does not like acid conditions, so add lime if necessary.

For an early supply of leaves, sow seeds in a cool greenhouse in February. Prick off into boxes, and transfer to the open ground in April.

Otherwise, sow outside in March or early April where the plants are to grow. The seed will take at least six weeks to germinate, so don't, as many gardeners do, give them up for lost and cultivate the soil. When they are through, thin them to about 15cm (6in) apart.

Seed can also be sown in July and covered with cloches to give a supply later in the year.

Keep the plants weed-free and

do not allow them to go short of water. Give them a feed with a nitrogen fertilizer when watering, to encourage the production of leaves.

Parsley is a biennial and will quickly go to seed in the second year. Remove any flower heads as they appear, or, better still, remove the plants altogether and sow another lot.

It will also do well inside in pots, and special ornamental parsley pots are available to make a decorative as well as useful display in the kitchen.

Preserving

Parsley can be dried, and this is generally done in a hot oven. It loses much of its flavour this way, however, and is better frozen. Sprigs can be frozen whole in plastic bags, and, when needed, they can be chopped before they are completely defrosted.

Uses

The uses of parsley are generally well known. Who has not eaten fish with a delicious parsley sauce? Chopped, it can be used on practically any dish and in salads and sandwiches. It can also be chopped and made into parsley butter. When chopped with shallots it becomes 'persillade' which should be added to dishes at the last minute so that it retains its flavour.

Rosemary
(Rosmarinus officinalis)

A hardy evergreen shrub that will grow in most situations, rosemary is highly aromatic and flavoursome. A native of the Mediterranean, it has been grown in this country for centuries. It is surrounded by folklore stories, supposedly being a great improver of the memory, and good for the head generally. Made into 'rosset sweetcakes', it was also said to 'make the heart merry'. It is still used widely at all sorts of ceremonies, and is placed on graves 'for remembrance'. It is also claimed to be an effective hair restorer and scalp tonic, and is still used in Greece to freshen clothes after washing.

Cultivation
Rosemary will withstand cold conditions, but hates bad drainage. It is best grown in soil that has been lightened with sand, and does particularly well against a warm wall. Given the right conditions it will grow into a bushy shrub some 3ft (1m) tall. It does tend to become rather leggy and untidy if neglected, and should therefore be trimmed back after flowering. Cutting the shoots for the kitchen will help to retain its compact shape.

Rosemary can be raised from seed sown in boxes in the spring. But it will be several years before the bushes reach usable size, so it is best to buy a bush and to propagate from that by cuttings. Take the cuttings from young growth off the main stem, in spring or early summer. The cuttings should be torn off rather than cut, to leave a 'heel' of bark from the main stem. Root them in pots or boxes in a cool greenhouse. Leave them in the greenhouse during the first winter and plant them out in May after hardening off.

Preserving
Since rosemary is evergreen, it will provide usable sprigs throughout the winter, so there is little point in preserving it. If, however, you

don't want to waste the clippings when the plants are cut back to prevent them becoming leggy, they can be dried. Hang them in bunches in a warm, airy spot out of direct sunlight. When they are quite dry, crumble them and put them into airtight jars.

Uses

Rosemary leaves have a delicious aroma when they are crushed. It is variously described as resembling ginger, pine, nutmeg and lavender, but really it is unique.

Sprigs of rosemary can be placed around and underneath many meat dishes—lamb, pork, veal, rabbit and poultry—to give them a delightful aroma and flavour. The stems do not soften during the roasting, so they must be removed before serving. They can however, be eaten, provided they are cut up before being added to vegetables, soups and fish dishes.

It should always be remembered that rosemary has a fairly pungent flavour that is not to everyone's taste. It is essential to use the herb with discretion, and not to allow it to swamp the natural flavour of the food it is meant to enhance.

Sage
(Salvia officinalis)

Sage is an old favourite with British cooks. It was also accredited with the ability to cure an amazing number of ills. Even today, there are many country folk who swear by a daily intake of sage, either in an infusion or eaten raw, in the belief that it prolongs life. Certainly many country folk live to a great age!

A hardy evergreen (or evergrey) shrub, it makes a decorative addition to the flower border, with its grey, velvety foliage and pretty violet-blue flowers.

Cultivation

Sage prefers a well-drained soil and full sun. It is worth preparing the ground for it before planting, by adding coarse grit to improve drainage on heavy soils. Like rosemary, it does have a tendency to become leggy and untidy. This can be counteracted by careful clipping. The leggy shoots can also be layered, by pegging them down into the soil. If a few nicks are made with a knife in the bark of the shoot, which is then pegged down with wire staples, it will root along its length. The plant can thus be induced to cover more ground, or the resulting plants can, after rooting, be detached from the parent plant and replanted.

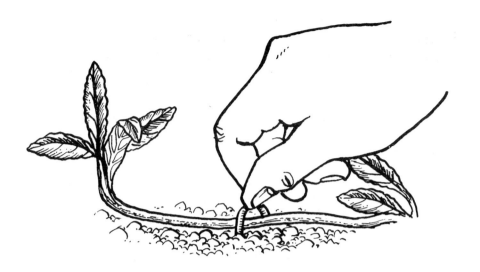

Layering shoots

Alternatively, plants can be raised from seed sown outside where the plants are to grow, in April. The seedlings will appear during May. When they are large enough to handle, they should be thinned out to leave them about 40cm (16in) apart.

Cuttings can also be taken in April or May. Take them with a 'heel', and root them in boxes in the greenhouse or in a frame.

After a few years, plants will lose vigour, and should be replaced. Sage can happily be grown in pots or tubs in full sun, though it will generally outgrow them in three or four years and will need to be replaced.

Preservation

Sprigs of sage can be dried, but they must be picked in the spring before the plants flower or the flavour will be impaired. Hang them in bunches in a warm, airy place out of direct sunlight. When dry, crumble them into airtight jars.

The leaves can also be successfully frozen. For short-term storage, pack the sprigs into polythene bags and freeze. For longer storage, the sprigs should be blanched in boiling water, dipped in cold water and then packed for freezing.

Uses

Perhaps the best-known culinary use is in sage and onion stuffing. It can also be used in sausages and pies, in cheese dishes and pea soup. It is also sometimes incorporated in pastry. The Italians use sage in conjunction with white wine in a delicious veal dish. Added to cream cheese in moderation, it makes a pleasant change from chives, and it can also be used to good effect with Welsh rarebit.

Bear in mind that sage has a pungent, spicy flavour, and so should be used with caution.

Savory

Summer Savory
(Satureia hortensis)
Winter Savory
(Satureia montana)

Summer savory is a rather loose, floppy annual, while winter savory is perennial and more erect. It is evergreen and forms an attractive small bush about 30cm (1ft) high.

Summer savory is said to have a more subtle flavour, though many gardeners prefer the stronger taste of the winter variety. Both have the added advantage of attracting myriads of bees. The leaves, incidentally, are reputed to relieve wasp and bee stings if rubbed into the spot.

Cultivation

Savory prefers a sunny spot and a well-drained soil, so it is worth preparing the ground with a little coarse grit if the soil is heavy.

Summer savory can be raised from seed, sown where the plants are to grow. When the seedlings emerge, thin them to about 15cm (6in) apart. The yield from summer savory is not high, so allow plenty of plants.

Summer savory will, of course, provide fresh leaves only in the summer, and is killed by frost.

Winter savory can be raised from seed sown in August. Do not cover the seed—it will germinate better in the light. When the seedlings are large enough to handle, thin them to about 30cm (1ft) apart.

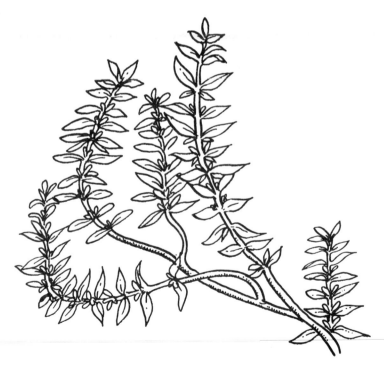

in bunches in a warm, airy spot, away from direct sunlight. When they are quite dry, crumble them and put them into airtight jars.

Uses

The traditional use for both types of savory is in bean dishes. The sprigs are put into the cooking water when it boils, and before serving, fresh young leaves can be chopped over the beans.

It is also widely used in pork and veal dishes and with grilled tomatoes and mushrooms. Added to salads, it gives a distinctive taste, particularly with cucumber and new salad potatoes.

The Germans use savory extensively to flavour trout, and the French use it in many types of sausage. Try it also with sautéed courgettes, for a quite different taste.

The flavour of savory is rather reminiscent of thyme, and it can be used as a substitute in any dishes where thyme is generally used.

Bear in mind that winter savory has a much stronger flavour than the summer variety, so it should always be used with caution.

Plants can also be raised from cuttings taken in late spring and rooted in a sandy soil outside.

Though it is a perennial, older plants do tend to lose vigour, so it is best to lift and split off the younger offsets on the outside of the crown. The older centre should be discarded and the younger offsets transplanted.

Winter savory makes a good edging plant and it will do well in pots or tubs.

Preservation

Winter savory, of course does not need to be preserved since leaves will be available throughout the summer and winter.

Summer savory dries well. Pick the young sprigs, and hang them

Sorrel

French Sorrel
(Rumex scutatus)
Broad-leaved Sorrel
(Rumex acetosa)

Sorrel is a sharp-tasting herbaceous perennial which must be used with a little discretion. The broad-leaved variety, particularly, contains high levels of oxalic acid, so you should never eat too much at one sitting, especially if you suffer from gout! Even so, the French used to eat it in prodigious quantities in much the same way as we eat spinach. It is supposed to be good for the digestion and for the blood and kidneys, though some authorities suggest that in fact the reverse is true. The claim that it is a stimulant to the appetite is probably better founded.

Apart from the cultivated varieties, sorrel can be found growing wild in Britain. The flavour of the wild variety is, however, much inferior to the cultivated types.

Cultivation
Sorrel prefers a rich, moist soil and will do well in partial shade. The soil should be prepared beforehand, by digging deeply and incorporating well-rotted farmyard manure or compost.

It can be raised from seed sown in April, but it will take a considerable time to produce a plant of usable size. Sow where the plants are to grow, and thin them to 30cm (1ft) apart when the seedlings are large enough to handle.

For quicker results, either buy a plant from which you can produce more later, or beg a root. The roots should be planted in the prepared soil in autumn, 30cm (1ft) apart.

During the season, keep the plants free from weeds and never let them go short of water. All flower stems should be removed as soon as they are seen, to encourage the production of new young leaves. Pick them over hard, and they will respond by producing new leaves quite quickly. In the winter, the leaves will die down, but they will re-appear early in spring.

After a few years, the plants will lose vigour, so it is best to lift them

and divide the roots every four years or so. The young outside roots should be replanted, and the older centres discarded.

Before the winter sets in, a few roots should be lifted and potted up. Brought into the cool greenhouse or on the kitchen windowsill, they will provide fresh leaves all winter. Alternatively, a few plants can be covered with cloches outside.

Preservation

The leaves can be dried. Pick them and lay them flat in a warm airy spot out of direct sunlight. When they are quite dry, crumble them into airtight jars. Sorrel does not freeze well fresh, but can be made into a purée and then frozen.

Uses

Sorrel soup is a renowned dish, particularly on the continent. The leaves can be used fresh in salads or chopped up and sprinkled on omelettes or scrambled egg.

The leaves can also be used cooked with vegetables, or wrapped round meat where they act as a tenderizer as well as flavouring.

Sorrel should be cooked in an enamel saucepan, because the oxalic acid combines with iron.

Tarragon
(Artemesia dracunculus)

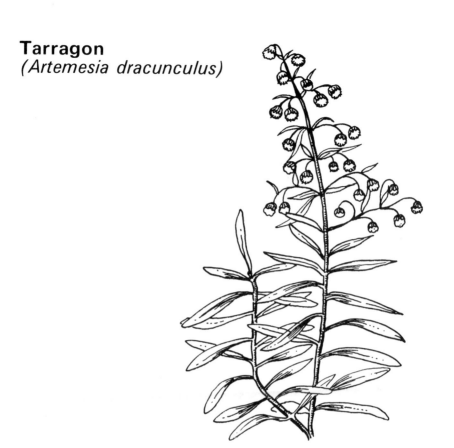

There are two types of tarragon, French and Russian. Though they look fairly similar, there is a great difference in flavour when used in the kitchen. Russian tarragon is either quite flavourless, or is so fierce that it makes food almost inedible. It is nonetheless sometimes used as a substitute for the French variety because it is much hardier and easier to grow.

French tarragon, on the other hand, has been described as the 'king of herbs'. Its flavour is quite unlike any other, being sweet but with an underlying suggestion of pepperiness. When the leaves are bruised, it is intensly aromatic. It is really the only type worth growing unless conditions are quite impossible.

French tarragon will grow to about 75cm (2½ft), and bears long, narrow, tender leaves of pale green.

Cultivation
Unfortunately, French tarragon cannot be grown from seed, and plants, which have to be propagated from cuttings, tend to be relatively expensive.

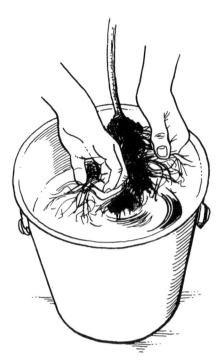

The easiest way to unravel tangled roots is in a bucket of water

time, they can be split to provide more plants. The roots have a habit of twining round each other in a most tortuous way. They should be carefully unravelled, rather than being cut or pulled apart. An easy way to do this is in a bucket of water.

Preservation

Tarragon dries quite well, though it will lose most if not all of its delicate aroma. Cut the sprigs early in the year and hang them in bunches in a warm, airy spot out of direct sunlight until they are quite dry. They can then be crumbled into airtight jars.

They can also be frozen, either straight into polythene bags, or, for longer storage, after blanching. Alternatively, freeze them after chopping them into ice-cube trays.

The plants prefer a sunny sheltered situation and a well-drained soil. Though it is a good idea to incorporate some organic matter, the soil should not be made too rich.

Planting is best carried out in the spring, setting the plants about 45cm (1½ft) apart. Make sure that the plants remain weed-free and never let them go short of water. They are described as evergreen perennials, but they are liable to lose their leaves and die back in winter. In colder areas, it is wise to protect the roots with a light covering of straw or bracken.

Plants should be lifted and re-planted every four years. At this

Uses

Most good cooks regard tarragon as an absolute essential to the success of many foods. It is often made into a flavoursome sauce, which is served with boiled chicken to produce a world-renowned dish. It goes very well with fish, used either in a sauce or in a stuffing. The young leaves can be chopped into salads and soups or on potatoes, mushrooms, game, seafood, liver and kidneys. It is an essential ingredient of the renowned Bearnaise sauce.

Whole sprigs can be used to flavour roast chicken, placing them inside with a crushed clove of garlic before cooking.

Tarragon vinegar is another use for this versatile and indispensable herb.

Thyme

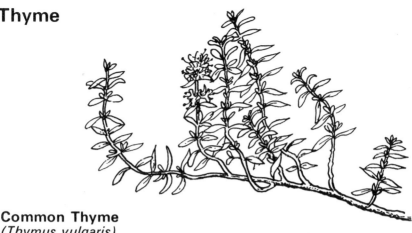

Common Thyme
(Thymus vulgaris)
Lemon Thyme
(Thymus citriodorus)

Thyme is undoubtedly one of our oldest and most popular herbs. There are many types, from the well-known rock garden plants to those used for making lawns. Common and lemon thyme are the only two used extensively in the kitchen.

Naturally, in the case of such an old herb, folklore abounds. Thyme was an essential ingredient of a concoction used to help the partaker to see fairies in the Middle Ages, while even further back, the Greeks associated it with both courage and grace.

A small, shrubby perennial, it will enhance the herb garden with its lilac flowers, and will attract bees and butterflies.

Cultivation
Thyme requires a light, well-drained spot, which should be well limed as it hates acid soil.

Common thyme can easily be raised from seed sown in a warm corner in April. When the seedlings emerge, thin them to 30cm (12in) apart. Lemon thyme, unfortunately, does not set seed.

Both plants, however, can be propagated from cuttings or by dividing the roots. For cuttings, pull off new young growth to leave a 'heel'. The cuttings should be about 5cm (2in) long, and should be rooted round the edge of a pot of sandy compost or in a cold-frame where a little sand has been added to the soil.

Alternatively, since these plants will tend to straggle, they can be increased by layering. Simply peg down shoots into the soil after having made a slight nick in the bark underneath. Once they have rooted they can be detached from the parent.

To encourage bushy growth and to prevent straggling, it is wise to cut the plants back hard in June, though pinching back the young shoots for the kitchen will help. Thyme is well suited to growing in pots or tubs.

Preserving
This is one of the few herbs where the dried leaves are more aromatic than the fresh ones. Cut the sprigs before the plant flowers and hang them in bunches in a warm airy spot out of direct sunlight. When they are quite dry, rub the leaves from the stems and store them in airtight jars.

Alternatively, the sprigs can be frozen in polythene bags, or, for longer storage, blanched in boiling water and then frozen.

Uses
Thyme is highly aromatic and supposedly good for the digestion. Lemon thyme is preferred by some cooks as it has a more fruity, less dominating flavour. It is used particularly in meat balls and other meat dishes, as well as baked custard.

Common thyme is more often used in stuffings and casseroles.

Both can be used fresh or dried, shredded on to salads, soups and fish dishes. It is delicious on vegetables such as aubergines, tomatoes, carrots and beetroot. It is, of course, an essential ingredient of bouquet garni.

It should always be remembered that thyme, especially common thyme, has a strong, pervading flavour, so it should be used sparingly. Properly used, it will enhance many dishes.

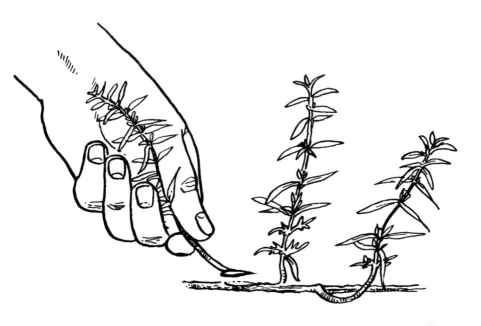

When taking cuttings, pull off the shoots to leave a 'heel'

Illustrated by Barry Gurbutt

Hamilton, Geoff
Herbs and how to grow them.—(Penny
pinchers).
1. Herb gardening
I. Title   II. Series
635′.7   SB351.H5
ISBN 0-7153-7897-X

Printed in Great Britain
by A. Wheaton & Co., Exeter
for David & Charles (Publishers) Limited
Brunel House   Newton Abbot   Devon

Published in the United States of America
by David & Charles Inc
North Pomfret   Vermont 05053   USA